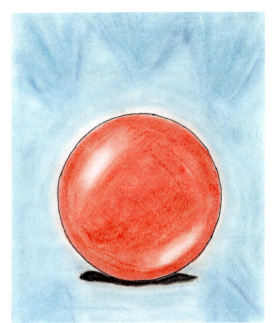

Always love
each other ♥
Debra & Ron
xoxo

To Christopher, Alexander & Sofia - σ' αγαπώ

First Published 2020

Text © 2002 Debra L. Pirsos

Illustrations © 2020 Dylann Rhea

All rights reserved. No part of this book may be reproduced in any form or by any means, electronic or mechanical, including photocopying, recording, or by an information storage and retrieval system, without permission in writing from the publisher.

ISBN 978-1-7357679-0-1

www.bunburysbooks.com

Breakfast With Papou

A Gastronomical Grandparenting Book

Written by Debra L. Pirsos

Illustrations by Dylann Rhea

BUNBURY'S BOOKS
PIERMONT, N.Y.

For Christopher and his beloved Papou

It's Sunday.

It's a special day.

The sun peeks into Christopher's room.

He wakes up, stretches and jumps out of bed.

He washes his face, brushes his teeth, and gets dressed.

He bounces downstairs
to call his Papou.

"Hello Papou, I'm ready."
says Christopher excitedly.

"Okay **pashamu**,
I'll be right over." says Papou.

Mommy and Daddy put
on his coat and
pack his bag with
books and toys.

The doorbell rings.

"Good Morning Papou!"
"Good Morning **comademu**!" says Papou as he hugs Christopher.

They walk out the door as Mommy and Daddy wave goodbye.

"Eat a good breakfast!" yells Mommy.

A beep and a wave and off they go to the Arena Diner.

As Papou and Christopher
enter the diner,
they are greeted
by the owners, Mike and Gus,
and the waiters,
and the waitresses,
and
all the cooks
in the kitchen,
and especially Dimitri and Harry.

After sitting down at their
corner table,
the waitress approaches
with a smile.

"The usual?" she asks.

"The usual!" says Papou
with a wink.

Within an instant,

one by one,

and

cart by cart...

10

TEN

fluffy

stacked

syrupy

pancakes...

9

NINE

long strips

of

wavy

bacon...

EIGHT

round

plates

of

hot

scrambled

eggs...

SEVEN

tall

glasses

of

orange

juice...

6

SIX

enormous

pieces

of

French

toast...

5

FIVE

very

berry

blueberry

muffins...

FOUR

plump

red

strawberries...

3

THREE

huge

cinnamon

waffles...

2

TWO

slices of

yellow

buttered

toast...

and
ONE
gigantic
apple strudel...

ARRIVE
AT THEIR
TABLE!

They finish their breakfast with a giant fruit cup topped with a red cherry!

Papou and Christopher are fuller than full.

But before they leave, Papou takes out a very special shiny quarter from his pocket.

He puts it into the biggest gumball machine ever!

Christopher turns the dial,

click,

Click,

CLICK!

And out rolls
the biggest,
reddest, shiniest,
gigantic red gumball!

"It's my favorite color!"
squeals Christopher.

Papou asks the hostess for the special wrapping.

As Papou wraps the gumball and puts it into his pocket, he says, "Our secret, right?"

"Right Papou!" Christopher says with a wink.

They say goodbye
to the
cooks,
the waiters,
the waitresses
and the
owners saying:

"Yassou!"

Mommy asks Papou if Christopher
ate all of his breakfast.

"Not everything," says Papou
with a little sigh.

But, with a grin, he pulls the
gumball out of his pocket
and slips it into Christopher's hand.

As Papou leaves,

he turns to Christopher and says,

"Same time next week?"

"Same time next week Papou!"

"I love you!"

"And I love you too, comademu!"

replies Papou.

Greek Translations:

Πάπου - Papou - Grandfather

Γιαγιά - Yiayia - Grandmother

Γεια σου! - Yassou - Goodbye/Hello

Πασάμ / paşam - Pashamu/my pasha

Kamari mou/Comademu - Term of Endearment

Other Translations:

Burrp! - Burp

"I remember very well the mystique I felt watching Papou dive in and out of the kitchen at the diner where he worked. He always seemed to be laughing and smiling and in my five year old brain I thought he just volunteered at the diner because of how fun it was!" ~ Christopher

Hugs from Papou, kisses from Yiayia and giggles by Christopher - 2002

Write or draw
a happy memory here.

Author Debra L. Pirsos continues to pursue a lifelong dream of solidifying her thoughts onto paper and into the hands of young at heart readers. Debra is a Yoga & Meditation teacher who presently owns Bunbury's Coffee & Tea Shop in the Lower Hudson Valley. By way of words and images, Debra conveys that peace begins within, and she strives to share her knowledge and intuitive insights to spark others. **A Star's Wish** is her first published book followed by **Breakfast With Papou**, *Book I of the Gastronomical Grandparenting Series* based on the interactions between her own children and their multicultural Grandparents.
Photo credit: Nik Strangelove

Illustrator Dylann Rhea is also a writer, and author of Readers' Choice award winner **Tormented Soul.** With over a decade of creating stories, Rhea specializes in worldbuilding and storytelling, focusing especially on everything magical. With a unique voice, Rhea brings you into a fantastical world of faeries and fae-like creatures. Author Laura Del says, 'Dylann Rhea writes a story that is dark, filled with suspense, and is both fresh and original, leaving you with a nagging feeling of wanting more.' Rhea lives and works based out of her home in Florida where she illustrates children's books and spends most of her time out in the garden with her fairies.

The Gastronomical Grandparenting Book Series:

Breakfast with Papou
Spaghetti with Yiayia
Tea with Gramma
Popcorn with Pop

Made in the USA
Middletown, DE
10 November 2020